A Painful Gift

A Painful Gift

The Journey of a Soul with Autism

CHRISTOPHER GOODCHILD

DARTON · LONGMAN + TODD

First published in 2009 by
Darton, Longman and Todd Ltd
1 Spencer Court
140–142 Wandsworth High Street
London SW18 4JJ

ISBN 978–0–232–52758–2

A catalogue record for this book is available from
the British Library.

Designed and produced by Sandie Boccacci
Set in 10/13.5pt Utopia
Printed and bound in Great Britain by
Cromwell Press Group, Trowbridge, Wiltshire

*This book is dedicated to my son,
whose love has helped me to find freedom –
my love for you is as deep as
the deepest ocean.*

*This book is also for those whose stories
and cries for freedom will never be heard
nor come to light in their lifetime.*

Contents

*Love in action is a harsh and dreadful thing
compared with love in dreams.*

Fyodor Dostoyevsky

Foreword

A painful gift
a book that wounds and reveals.

The story of a gentle man
who is constantly lost
yet found.

Lost,
because he never knew
he was sick with autism.
But found,
when it was diagnosed many years on.

It was no longer then a sickness
but part of his being.
A way of life
his way of life
and of relating or of fleeing relationships.

Found and lost through relationships
found by Jesus
and by Daniel, his beloved son.

A moving, deeply moving story

that can reveal our woundedness but also our hope

how quickly we judge through the prism of our fears
and wounds.

Yet found by Jesus

who is always there – but so often silent.

Our hope.

JEAN VANIER
November 2008

Acknowledgements

IN THE NATIONAL GALLERY in London there hangs the famous Velázquez painting *Kitchen Scene in the House of Martha and Mary*. Although the techniques the artist used, as well as the message that he wished to convey, remained a mystery, what is obvious is that this seventeenth-century painting places Christ in the background, while the servant girl takes centre stage.

It is therefore fitting for me to refer to the imagery in this painting to acknowledge and thank my dear friend Katherine, who, like the servant girl in the picture, worked quietly behind the scenes of action, tirelessly helping me, and listening with such unfailing love that I trusted her to enter my world of autism. The love she has shown me remains as mysterious as the *Kitchen Scene in the House of Martha and Mary*. Not being a natural writer myself, it was only with her help that I have been able to give shape to my story. Because of the difficulties I have had all my life with writing, and because of the unusual and idiosyncratic ways in which I express myself, Katherine has taken great pains to understand and interpret my writing. Therefore virtually every line of the book has, in effect, been 'translated' by her to make it more accessible.

One of the ways I communicate is to remember

and then re-play as my own, phrases that I have read or heard. I have tried to tell my story in my words but if any unwitting plagiarism remains, I apologise.

I have changed some names, for reasons I think you will understand.

Thanks are also due

To Brian, Katherine's husband, who has shown me great kindness by helping to produce and edit all the drafts of my book.

To my adoptive parents and sister, who cared for me as best they could and taught me more than they will ever know.

To the mother of my son, and his brother and sister and grandparents for letting me into their lives and loving my son in a way that I can never come close to either offering or experiencing.

To my godmother, my very first friend in life.

To Patrick, who taught me the art of listening with love.

To Marek and Maria, for their friendship and hospitality.

To Father Pat, who has shown me endless kindness and support over the years.

To Kate Frost fcJ, who offers me spiritual direction from the goodness of her heart.

To Linda my psychotherapist, for illuminating my darkness.

To my brother Caspar, who designed my website and offered his technical skills.

To Annerie, a lovely and generous friend.

To Razz, who like my son brings me out into the light of the world.

To Jean Vanier, for his kind and deeply sensitive words in the Foreword of my book. His work with vulnerable people inspires me and will forever be an inspiration in my ministry.

To Gerard Hughes and Bronwen Astor for their kind words and endorsement of my book.

To Donna Williams, for endorsing my book. Her beauty and vision know no bounds. Through her work and through her spirit I am being led to a place of greater freedom.

To Julie Lonneman, for her permission to use her deeply inspiring illustrations which accompany my story so beautifully.

To Brendan Walsh, for his vision, sensitivity and gifts as an editor, without which my story would never have reached publication. And also to all the team at Darton, Longman and Todd.

To all my Aspie friends, who understand the long loneliness so well.

To all my friends in London, the Catholic Worker and fellow travellers everywhere.

CHRISTOPHER GOODCHILD
19 August 2008

INTRODUCTION

Your joy is your sorrow unmasked.

Kahlil Gibran

As FAR BACK AS I can remember, I recall a deep longing to enter into the unity of all things, and to connect deeply with the world around me. I ached not only to feel the sun on my face, the wind in my hair, and the smell of the garden in springtime – I longed to be one with them. It seemed mysterious to me then that the very things that brought me such joy would also bring me such pain. The sun and wind would bring blisters to my face, the may blossom would make my nose run and my eyes swell, and the kaleidoscope of colours would dazzle my eyes. It seemed I ached for what I could not bear.

When it came to the social world, I felt like a bewildered stranger, often drowning in a tidal wave of sensation. People, places and things would melt and blend like a surrealist painting. Words and sounds would scream at me and then like magic somehow melt away. Everything seemed transcendent and immanent all at once.

Welcome to my world. I have autism.

However, this book is not so much about my autism, but about the struggle to be truly myself in the world. To be fully human, to touch people and to be touched by people in return. As the Cistercian monk Thomas Merton once said, 'To be a saint is to be truly oneself.'

As a Christian I have always held a deep affinity with Jesus. When I first thought of writing my story, the Stations of the Cross offered me not only a useful structure for outlining my life with Asperger's syndrome, but also powerful imagery to accompany people along the journey that led to my diagnosis in the summer of 2007. For those unfamiliar with the Stations of the Cross, they represent points along the way of Jesus' last moments of his life, covering his trial, sentencing, crucifixion and resurrection and the people who came into contact with him at that time.

Asperger's syndrome is a high-functioning form of autism and falls within the autistic spectrum. It was first identified over fifty years ago by Hans Asperger, a Viennese paediatrician. I was in my early forties when I was formally diagnosed with it. The reason such an understanding of myself evaded me for so long will become clear as my story unfolds. In my story, I describe the life I led, unaware of my difference, and also my struggles with depression living in this 'cloud of unknowing' until my diagnosis, then I end with a reflection on how my outlook on life has subsequently changed so radically.

One way to describe a person with autism is someone who comes not from another planet, but rather from a different culture and who has a different way of perceiving our world.

Autism is a blessing, a gifted way of seeing the world. It is also deeply misunderstood. There is much talk today of finding a cure for autism, and even if that is remotely possible, I would have no interest in such cures, for the simple reason that there IS nothing wrong with me that needs curing. If anybody needs an immunising injection to shield against the crippling effects of their general predisposition, it is those who feel the need to fix individuals, societies, or whole cultures. For it is the inability to accept difference that cries out to be remedied.

However, although I regard autism as a gift, it can be a painful gift in many ways. Even producing this book has been painful, since writing has always been a distressing and uncomfortable experience for me because of my autism and dyslexia. It was an enormous strain physically, mentally and emotionally, so I regard the publication of this book as being a miracle in itself.

When I had nearly finished writing my story, and I realised that what I was writing might possibly find its way into the public domain, I became aware of the temptation to dampen down and sanitise the darker moments of my journey in order to make them more palatable to others. I resisted this temptation for the

most part, because I felt called to share my woundedness in full, so that others might be strengthened in
the process of bringing to light their woundedness too.

My deepest prayer is that all who read this book,
including my son, if he so wishes when he comes of
age, will be inspired to see that, as was the case in my
story, it is often that which gives us the deepest sorrow
in life that can bring us the greatest joy. It is for this
reason that my book is dedicated to my son, because,
despite all the difficulties regarding managing myself
when I was with him in the early years, the times I
spent with him were, and will remain, the greatest and
most joy-filled moments of my entire life.

Above all my son has taught me that great love and
great suffering are part of the spiritual journey, and
that it is only through great love and great suffering
that human beings can be transformed, for it is, I
believe, in my poverty and in my joy God resides. The
fact that love and joy bring me such intense pain can
only truly be understood by travelling deeply into my
inner landscape.

> *... We are put on earth a little space*
> *That we may learn to bear the beams of love.*
>   William Blake

Station 1
CONDEMNED

Jesus. How hard it is for me to be condemned, not by my difference, but by the world's indifference to my way of being that seems not of this world.

I was adopted at the age of six weeks from the Crusade of Rescue, which was a Catholic home for destitute mothers and their children. My adoptive parents came from working-class families and both grew up in North London during the Second World War. I had a sister, who was also adopted from the Crusade of Rescue; she was two years older than me. She was clearly different from me – she was talkative, I was quiet and learnt to talk later than the average child. In childhood photographs my sister is always beaming, but I have no trace of a smile. How to perform such a feat seemed totally beyond me.

When I was able to crawl I would struggle for dear life to be away from family members, only to be picked up and returned to them. Over and over again this painful ritual was re-enacted, painful because being held felt like what some people experience when they scrape their fingernails down a blackboard. The more I resisted my mother's attempts to cuddle me, the more she persisted. I soon realised the wisdom that comes with acceptance and in the end gave in to my mother's need to hold me, over my need to be away from her. It must have been hard for my mother to experience this rejection from me.

My earliest memories were of a world that felt totally overwhelming. Lights, sounds, movements and smells flooded into my senses, leaving me feeling distressed and anxious. For me it made perfect sense to remove myself from all social interaction. This way I felt safe from a world that was strange and alien to me, and the more I ventured out into the world the more I wanted to retreat from it. I soon learned that whenever I was able to shut my bedroom door behind me, all my problems just seemed to magically evaporate. How wonderful! What bliss!

One of my greatest difficulties was in understanding what people were saying to me, as everything was so confusing. I recall working tirelessly from an early age, creating sophisticated ways of communicating in order to cope. I built entire systems in my imagination – my brain was like a library filled with images and words. However, in order to gain access to this 'library', I needed more time than the world allowed. Only in isolation could the conditions be created whereby my system of thinking would operate.

I remember, around the age of three or four, being given one of those objects which was filled with water and which, when shaken, would make snowflakes swirl around in some scene or other. I was fascinated by this object – it seemed so much like me with all that frantic swirling movement going on while the main character remained so visibly unaffected within the hermetically sealed container. I would love the fact that I had complete control over the movement of the snow, and I loved the way the soft white flakes fell so gently to the ground. I saw myself as a snowflake and my parents as hard rocks that I would fall against and then melt. I ached for them to be snow like me, so we could be held together, held together in a field of snow.

Beyond the place of right and wrong, there is a field – I'll meet you there.

Rumi

Station 2

TAKING UP THE CROSS

Jesus. How hard it is for me to accept at times, that I am the way I am. So broken, vulnerable and so susceptible to seeking love from others and not from that part of me that reaches out to you. I accept this as my cross. Help me. Help me to get out of the way of your loving grace.

'WAKE UP, CHRIS. Is there anybody there?'

'He is in a world of his own.'

'Chris is not concentrating and appears not to be in the world at all.'

These were typical examples of my school reports as a child. I found school totally overwhelming. When the teachers spoke, their words echoed and repeated themselves in my mind, which was very confusing. Information had no meaning or significance. I couldn't remember what the teacher said because I was too agitated. I couldn't cope with written work at all. I had difficulty learning to write and my handwriting was very untidy – the letters often came out back to front and I couldn't write on the lines. I often couldn't read what I had written. I was never able to do any home-work because I couldn't remember what to do and I was too distressed. Having such serious learning difficulties was no fun. In fact it was soul-destroying being bottom of the class year after year, and being thought of as not caring. In fact I cared deeply, but was too fearful and bewildered to find a way of expressing myself to the world.

My earliest memory of school was in kindergarten and the teachers asking me to leave the class and do painting in a separate room. Such was the level of dis-tress I felt at being completely overwhelmed by my inability to concentrate, that I became too agitated and fidgety to remain in the classroom.

Life at home was no easier. I felt terribly misunderstood by my mother who had started to drink heavily, and began telling me that I was behaving in an odd manner, and that I had to 'act more normal'. I think she often overheard me having conversations with myself in my room, and she would have also heard the various creative sounds I produced with my voice, in order to experience the pleasure that came from the vibrations in my head.

Social situations filled me with such intense anxiety, that I was totally unable to engage with an authentic sense of self, or participate most of the time without rigid control over my anxieties and behaviour. Often my way of managing myself in these situations was to hide or quietly wander off. This was my only way in which I could find the freedom to be myself. An unwritten rule seemed to emerge in my family, that 'Chris does not do social things'. I think I was often seen as selfish and inconsiderate, though I was always very polite.

To my parents, my preoccupation with objects and attachments to my toys, as well as my social exclusion, odd quirks, tics etc., not only seemed odd but also a threat to the family image, which everyone seemed to have a great interest in upholding. As a result, my difficulties were seen as something that needed to be 'got rid of' through harsh discipline because my very 'being me' was seen as an act of defiance against my parents' accepted standards of behaviour.

Even my appearance did not come up to their standards of middle-class respectability. A lot of the time I looked quite scruffy because the clothes I was expected to wear felt horribly uncomfortable, stiff and constricting, and the material they were made of, and the labels inside them, used to irritate my skin. This was especially true of my school uniform: I just couldn't bear my school tie tight round my neck. I could hardly wait to get out of formal clothes so I could wear something more comfortable and less restricting. I hated my clothes. I also hated having my hair cut. My father, who was very particular about how it looked, used to comb it for me, but I used to wriggle and wouldn't sit still long enough for him to tidy it up properly. The lotion he would put on it to smooth it down used to sting my scalp terribly.

My anxiety was unbearable at times, as my rigid routines and ways of managing myself in the world were condemned by my mother as mad, odd and disrespectful. When I was on my own I used to comfort myself by talking to myself, by making noises and by going round my room stroking things, smelling things and touching myself, especially my head. These were things I had to conceal from my family, and conform as best I could in order to avoid being humiliated.

Most nights when my parents went to bed, and when they woke in the mornings, they argued. Their

bedroom door was opposite mine. I would put my ear
to their door, and listen to my mother talking inces-
santly, often screaming hysterically about how insane
and affected I was.

At the time I did not know how seriously unwell my
mother was, so her talking about me in this way deeply
unsettled and unhinged me and gave me a fear of
being mad which has haunted me ever since. My
father had great difficulty supporting me, choosing
instead to just listen my mother out. This pained me,
for I ached for my father to stop her hurting me. It was
in these moments with my ear to my parents' door, I
could feel myself entering into the world Thomas
Hardy offers us when he said,

> Childlike, I danced in a dream,
> Blessings emblazoned that day;
> Everything glowed with a gleam;
> Yet we were looking away.

I was splitting in two. Feeling totally defeated, I
retreated ever more deeply into my secret world.

I remember kissing my favourite toys and then
tying them up with strong cotton or string, and throw-
ing them out of the window. However, I did have every
intention of salvaging them after the great sacrifice,
that is, if they survived. Some never did and they got
lost for ever. I remember once, one of my favourite
toys got stuck on the roof below my bedroom window.

I panicked, and jumped out of the window crashing straight through the asbestos roof and landing on the floor below. I don't remember feeling any pain whatsoever as my body crashed to the floor, and my head and shoulders took the full force of the landing.

When I picked myself up and walked back indoors, my mother was washing up. She looked at me, saying 'Why are you looking so disgracefully filthy?' To which I replied in a monotone and with a rather affected manner, something like, 'I appear to have fallen through the roof, and it seems I have done some considerable damage, mother.' In response to this I was told to go to my room until my father returned from work and tidy up my room because it was a disgrace. My mother must have thought I was just fooling around and I was unable to convey to her how I felt; it was impossible to get her to believe me.

My mother seemed so sad to me; I so wished she could accept me for being so sensitive, and yet my quiet and aloof ways, my very being me, seemed to pose a great threat to her. 'Why do you have to be so abnormal?', 'Why do you take such great delight in acting odd all the time?' and, worst of all, 'You are destroying my life – wait till your father gets home!' That one hurt me the most, because I hated the thought that it was I who was making my mother's life so miserable. All this seemed in such stark contrast to the mother who was at times able to be gentle and attentive, when we would say prayers together at night-time. Although my mother was brought up in an Irish Catholic home, she had little desire for the faith any more, yet I recall times of great tenderness saying the Hail Mary together on occasions at bedtime.

Living in a family that was so driven to be normal at all costs was a great strain on everyone, not only myself. This resulted in my adapting and creating many skills to face the world with a convincing façade of normality. I learnt to master the art of simulating normality to such an extent that I learnt to conceal almost all visible traits of affectedness such as tics, blinking quickly or slowly, touching, odd quirky sounds etc. However, I just did these things when no one was around, and had the ability to conceal my many quirks and unusual habits for the best part of the day, that is, until I got home and entered my room. And then, as soon as I gently shut the door behind me, my little body would melt, and I would become one again.

I must have been so hard for my parents, for my actions seemed to imply I did not want to be with them. The truth was, I just did not know how to be with them.

Station 3

FALLING DOWN

Jesus. Be in my thoughts and actions today. But if my thinking escapes you and I fall, lead me back to you, as gently as a feather falls unto a feather, gently lead me unto you.

THE WEIGHT ON MY SHOULDERS was fast proving too great for me to bear. By the age of seven I remember feeling gloomy, unhappy and alone. This was the first time I remember thinking, 'What's the point in trying if I never get anywhere?' My school reports continued to show I was deeply withdrawn and fast becoming unreachable and unteachable. An educational psychologist assessed me with a view to evaluating my suitability for education in a public school. As his report said my IQ was above average, the message was to pull my weight and knuckle down.

My mother's depressive condition got worse, and the daily humiliation at home continued unabated. I started counting obsessively and realigning my toys in symmetry over and over again. Also I would often hide in my room and create new personas and characters from listening to the radio or from watching films. This equipped me with certain skills in order to avoid being seen as odd at home and in school. I was teaching myself social graces, like an actor preparing myself for a play.

At this time, I recall an incident where my mother was aggressively cleaning the family dog, the steel comb digging into his skin. I remember hearing his muffled whimpers (all the family's dogs learned to dampen down their cries as my mother would beat her fist in the dog's face if it showed any defiance), and seeing his pathetic eyes so beaten, and watching my mother's face all contorted, as the sharp teeth cut into his scrotum. Just hearing his cries broke me. These awful displays of such insensitivity would be carried out quite openly. No one really challenged my mother, especially not me. I was mute. But deep inside me I cried, and felt absolute outrage for her callous insensitivity, and guilt for my complicity.

I formed close relationships with all the family dogs, simply because we were the scapegoats for my mother's desperate inability to manage her anger. It was by looking into our dogs' eyes that I learned empathy. Empathy is easy if it is in close proximity to my own pain. Also to be touched deeply by another opens my heart to love. I wanted so much to love all the dogs we had. We always only had one dog at a time, and the dogs were my only friend. I let them into my secret world.

When I came out of my secret world I was a broken and fragmented person. I had refined my characters sufficiently well – enough to shield myself from much of my mother's wrath, and from the awkwardness of being seen as overtly anxious in social situations or at school. Subsequently I never experienced life through a real sense of self, but through these very characters that I created in order to protect my hidden self. My body felt trapped and locked into itself like a frozen object, and at times, when I had to be in the company of other children, I felt like a scarecrow in the midst of a playground full of screaming children. Only through *Macbeth* can I find the words to convey this experience:

> Give sorrow words; the grief that does not speak,
> Whispers the o'er-fraught heart, and bids it break.

And yes, my heart was broken into many pieces by the loneliness of being so cut off from myself and the world around me.

By the time I was around eleven I developed an all-consuming interest in Subbuteo football, which was a very popular indoor football game in the seventies, and I had numerous teams in my collection. I played this game with total absorption, and only came out of my room to eat or go to the toilet. I developed whole structures of leagues and super-leagues and all the players had characters and personalities of their own, which I had learnt to emulate through watching *Match of the Day* on the television. I would play this game for hours on end after school and all the time at week-ends. Despite my parents' insistence that I should make friends and spend less time on my own, I very rarely made the effort, because the effort of sustaining such contact with someone was so great that I could not see the point in friendship at all. All my free time was spent playing alone.

At this time I vividly recall experiencing the awful fear of death, and believed that death could come to me at any time. When this fear became all-consuming, my thoughts would speed up to such an extent, that the only way I could slow them down, was to swallow and count obsessively and unrelentingly, until I had forgotten the feelings that were upsetting me.

Station 4

MOTHER

*Jesus. My heart is a lonely hunter. From the lips of my wounds
I pray to you and your mother. For in my darkest moments I
have no one else to turn to. When I am being crushed like
grapes, I am unaware of the wine I will become, but through
my tears I can also taste the pain of those who hurt me —
how sweet those tears!*

ALL MY LIFE I had ached for someone to save me. I recall hanging around the shops waiting for a woman – my natural mother possibly – to save me, someone who could give me the unconditional love and warmth I had been deprived of from early childhood. But no mother came along to offer me the love and emotional support I longed for. Nobody came into my world and ever saw me, and deeply understood me. I ached for love, to be loved and to be understood.

I found summertime particularly distressing. As spring approached, my sense of smell would be overwhelming, but the beauty of spring and summer's glory would just seem to mock my intense desperation and bring to light the darkness in my soul.

Around the age of twelve, it was decided that I would go to boarding school. I rather liked the idea. The thought of getting away from my parents and their humiliation of me for being different was very attractive to me. However, the experience only lasted a couple of months, as not being able to have space to myself drove me into awful anxiety states. I had no door to shut away the world. I became flooded with fear and was bullied and punished most nights due to my inability to sleep. Because there was no private space to organise my characters, I could not hide my awkwardness and eccentric behaviour and was frequently punished for being different. It seemed the only thing I was a great success at was turning up on time for classes, so punctuality assumed enormous importance for me. I was always present in body, regardless of whether or not I was totally absent in mind.

I loved football; it was my saving grace in my prep school that took great pride in its pupils' academic achievements. I was good at playing it too, and although on the field, as well as off it, my communication skills were very poor, I made up for it by sheer determination, will-power and love of the game. It was also a great opportunity to let out some of the aggression that was building up inside me. However, I had to leave the school because of a series of humiliating incidents that left the teachers and my parents alike convinced that a more gentle and sensitive approach to my education would be best for me.

I went to many schools, but was always deeply unhappy. I was often taken advantage of and bullied, but my unusual and creative ways would often be appreciated by the more sensitive and artistically minded pupils.

I also had the opportunity to follow my interest in football out of school too. My father was the club doctor of the local non-league side. I soon developed an obsessive interest in the club, and would follow the team with my father for many years. It was here, in the rusty corrugated iron stands, that my dreams came true. I felt alive. I felt deeply happy. For it was here that I would experience joy and sadness spontaneously with my father. These memories I treasure.

At the age of fifteen, I got into trouble with the police. I felt so misunderstood and angry at being daily humiliated that my actions were a desperate cry for the help I was not getting at home. I enjoyed copying other people, imitation playing a very important part in trying to relate to, and interact with, others. There was a boy who lived in the same street as me who used to spray racist graffiti on the shopfront of a shop-keeper he was targeting. Impressionable and com-pliant, and without realising that I was being taken advantage of, I was persuaded by him to do this too. Also, after hearing on the news about a man who sent hoax bombs and threatening letters, I thought it would please my friend if I did the same. So I put some bits of Lego in an envelope and sent it to the same shop-keeper. Unaware of any distress my actions might be causing, after hearing on the television the following week about how the Yorkshire Ripper used to cut out letters from newspapers and stick them in his letters to his victims, I did it as well. However, I got caught by the local policeman and was arrested and charged with threatening to kill, sending hoax bombs and criminal damage. It felt rather good that the spotlight was turned on me for the first time in my life. He was a nice policeman who arrested me and interviewed me at the local police station. I took full responsibility for what I had done, seeing it as being all my own fault. A strong sense of loyalty to my friend meant that I never told anyone who else was involved and he was never caught. I was found guilty on all three charges. The consequences of this never occurred to me at the time – a criminal record for life.

The arrest turned my life upside down. My difficulties had been getting worse at home and at school, I was not eating and was unable to sleep. It was as a result of my arrest that I was sent to one of the main teaching hospitals in London for an assessment by a consultant psychiatrist.

I will never forget seeing this doctor for the first time. My mind was ablaze with anxious thoughts, such as 'Will I be sectioned?', 'Will I be condemned as mad?' In fact when I saw him for the first time I felt very comforted. He had a kind face, rather pompous looking, but his soft and gentle features I found very disarming. He was a man in his early sixties, clearly very well educated and with much experience in child psychiatry. I spent a little time with him on my own that first session, whilst my parents were asked to leave the consulting room. Afterwards I was left with this feeling that he was on my side.

Within a month or so I was admitted to the hospital where this doctor worked. I was put on a cocktail of anti-psychotic medications that rendered my time in hospital a 'wipe-out' for the most part. On a daily dose of 150 mg of Chlorpromazine plus other drugs such as

Imipramine and Procyclidine (a drug used for people with Parkinson's disease in order to manage the debilitating side-effects), I was being treated for schizophrenia. I felt I was in the bowels of hell. My jaw ached and my ability to control certain bodily functions was greatly impaired. Along with my fears, my hopes and dreams all seemed to be squeezed and pushed down as if in a hermetically sealed cafetière. The medication ensured there was no movement towards healing. Nothing was being solved; all my problems were being 'packed away'.

The only redeeming feature of my stay in the hospital was my twice-weekly sessions with the doctor I had first seen. Throughout my hospitalisation, the doctor became larger than life for me. He paid me great compliments, and although most of them centred on my looks, I was oblivious to the life-changing implications this would have on both of us later on. I never foresaw how it would complicate the therapeutic value of my being in his care at the time. All I felt was what I perceived as love. Our sessions together always made me feel happy, because I really felt that, at last, someone out there thought I was worth something.

The hospital I was in was a typical Victorian psychiatric institution, with its long crumbling corridors and well-planned garden displays. From my bedroom window I would watch the patients wandering like ghosts around the circular walkways. I recognised a well-known comedian in the ward next to mine and from my window I could see him and the other patients rocking to and fro to the rhythm of their medicated thoughts.

It is a terrible thing to see human beings so lost and possessed so completely. And yet I became fascinated with the many patients I would see wandering around the grounds. Although some patients looked like walking ghosts, pale and motionless from the waist upwards, others looked more like walking hurricanes, waving their arms around as if they were being attacked by a swarm of bees. I felt such compassion for the people there, many of them so gentle and deeply sensitive like myself. I feel it was here that I learned to listen and to observe the human condition at its greatest depth. Rainer Maria Rilke clearly knew something of this experience, when he said,

> Only he who has eaten
> poppies with the dead
> will not lose ever again
> the gentlest chord.
> … Inside the double world
> all voices become
> eternally mild.

The smell of the hospital filled me with horror. It was an assault on my senses, but I only became aware of how repugnant the smell was when I would return to the hospital after my weekend visits to my parents. It was deeply unsettling to go away from the hospital and then return again. I felt disorientated, and each time I arrived back at the hospital I felt this profound sense of coming home to where home could never be found.

Because of the powerful medication I was on, I remember very little else of my stay. My body felt as if it had been filled with glue, and that this glue was sticking me together. I ached for things to fall apart, so each part could be tended, so that I could be built anew. I craved to feel the wind on my cheeks, the sun on my face and to know what it felt like to kiss a woman tenderly on the lips.

I left the hospital after nearly eighteen months of being an inpatient. How good it felt to have survived! How good it felt to know I would be free, free of the hard, paranoid and untrusting eyes of the staff, whose job, it seemed, was little more than being a jailer to us all.

I had a formal arrangement to continue seeing the doctor after my discharge. I was still living at home at this time, and would see him fortnightly in his London apartment. On one of our first sessions here, I recall talking about how I felt that I needed to leave home, because my mother's ill health was getting worse. As I was going into detail about how she was threatening me with a knife, all of a sudden I recall him breaking in saying, 'Stop! Hold that face, don't move.' Then from somewhere he pulled out a camera and took a photo of me, asking me to freeze a certain expression. This left me feeling angry with him for the first time, for I thought, 'Is he more interested in my face than my feelings?'

Over the following two years, the camera would become a major feature in our sessions, and would eventually lead to me having to take all my clothes off and watch pornographic videos with him. This led in turn to sexual contact between us. I felt outraged and bitterly let down and yet powerless to stop him, because I felt that if I were to say no, he would condemn me as mad and send me back to the hospital.

This relationship ended tragically. After I had entered psychotherapy in my mid-twenties and was able to start the process of feeling the feelings that had resulted in me splitting off and disassociating, I challenged the doctor to confront his neglect of my care and his violation of me. He panicked, fearing his life and reputation would be ruined, and he committed suicide. The man who, I thought, was the kind and loving father I craved, was in fact a man who was, like me, unable to form healthy loving relationships, which had resulted in him abusing boys in his care. For many years after he killed himself I felt guilty and responsible for his death, and the enormity of its implications still deeply unsettles me to this day.

His suicide was a defining moment in my life. The way in which this news was broken to me was very dramatic. I had left home by then, so my mother and father asked me to come home as they wanted to tell me something. Their tone told me that something very serious had occurred. When they explained the situation, there was real fear and anxiety on their faces. When they told me what their fear was, I knew then that my whole family's meaning for existence was under threat. My parents made me promise that I would keep this story a deep secret. The reason they gave was my sister's career. 'If the news got out,' said my mother, 'your sister's career would be destroyed overnight.'

The little boy in me screamed, 'How dare you think of my sister's needs and those of your own at this time. How dare you. How bloody dare you both!' However, all that was able to come out of my lips was, 'All right. I promise I won't say anything.'

I went back to my flat that night in a thousand pieces. I can remember the terror I felt that the police would ring at my door in the middle of the night, and arrest me for the doctor's death, or that I would go mad with the feelings that were exploding within me. The gentle words of George Appleton sum up beautifully my desperate hopes that night, as I fell asleep feeling more alone in the world than ever before.

Give me a candle of the spirit, O God, as I go down into the depths of my being. Show me the hidden things, the creatures of my dreams, the storehouse of forgotten memories and hurts. Take me down to the spring of my life, and tell me my nature and my name. Give me freedom to grow, so that I may become that self, the seed of which you planted in me at my making. Out of the depths I cry to you, O God.

I ached to be listened to, yet I had no idea what I was holding on to, for denial can run as deep as the deepest ocean, for reasons that I was soon to fully understand and deeply respect much later.

Station 5

BEING HELPED

Jesus. How we all give and receive love so imperfectly!
To listen with love is a rare gift indeed.

I HAD LEFT HOSPITAL with deep relief. Although my childhood trauma remained unexplored due to the complicated issues surrounding my relationship with the doctor, I was pleased to be back in the world, even though I was oblivious to how my ways of conformity, and concealment regarding my anxieties, would handicap me later on in life, with further depression, problems with employment and difficulties with relationships. I had frequent nightmares about my time in hospital, and still do, as well as trauma reactions to visiting doctors and hospitals

I was soon to have my first serious relationship with a woman, and it was an awful shock to my system, as I had unconsciously always associated intimacy with feelings of outrage and violation. Trust was impossible for me to experience. Naomi was a very beautiful Egyptian woman whom I met at Speakers' Corner. We were both in our early twenties, and shared a love of folk music and folk festivals.

After a couple of weeks Naomi moved into my flat in Kensal Green and we lived together for over three years, before the relationship came to a stormy end with much sadness and bitterness. The anxiety I had around managing the relationship was immense. How could it not be? I had no sense of self, only a shell and a handful of personas at my disposal. Subsequently I would suffer from ongoing bouts of depression and nervous exhaustion. Because of the extreme stress, I started having problems controlling my vocal and facial tics. I cried with the anxiety of feeling so redundant in love. It was because of this feeling of redundancy at the core of my being, that I entered the world of psychotherapy.

After all that I had gone through, I was naturally questioning, and extremely cautious, with regard to whom I was prepared to work with in therapy. I knew very little about all the many different approaches and schools of thought. However, I was prepared to shop around until I found something I felt comfortable with.

There were now certain conditions which had to be met, in order for me to be able to open up my soul to someone. Not that I had too much of a clue what I had to open up. However, I knew certain things could not be compromised. Firstly, he or she had to be able to look at me like a human being, and not like the many bearded and frightened functionaries of the psycho-analytical institutions, of which I was most certainly a casualty. I craved gentleness, compassion and under-standing, and because of the abuse by the doctor, I needed to be reassured that the therapist was not working out of a place of unfreedom in themselves.

I soon found someone whom I liked. She was a very elderly woman, trained in the Jungian tradition, who lived on the edge of Hampstead Heath. After a couple of sessions I felt quite at home with this wise Jungian therapist. I was impressed by her contemplative presence and profound understanding of the human condition. There was also a quality of great tenderness in her that left me feeling I could take the risk of trusting her. Subsequently, it did not take long before I was able to get in touch with my anger, and it soon became clear to me that anger was the only energy that could pierce the veil of shame that had held me hostage all these years. Perhaps it was for this reason why, as a child, I loved that beautifully cathartic and anarchic quality inherent within the punk movement, for in some way I knew then that anger, if it could find its rightful home, could lead me to freedom. All the positive thinking and affirmations work I had done in recent months now looked as if I was just rearranging the deckchairs on the *Titanic*. I was on a collision course.

This wise old lady knew well that I had just hit an iceberg, and I was sinking fast, my life being thrown overboard. My personas, characters, everything seemed to be floating in an angry and violent sea that threatened to take me under. We worked together for what seemed like an eternity, piecing back together the fragments of my splintered self. However, the work proved too much for her and I needed to find a therapist who specialised in the field of childhood trauma and its associated conditions. I needed to go deeper, deeper than I sensed she was able to bear herself.

I worked for many years with two more therapists on this painful material spanning many years. The work was invaluable in reclaiming my feelings, and the grieving process was intense and went on for many years. The tears were heavenly; it was the most profound contemplative experience I have ever had. However, psychology could only go so far in giving me complete answers to the mystery of my true self.

I traced my natural father at this time too. He was a talented artist, a gift he had inherited from his mother, who was a very successful and well-known sculptor. I was so excited to discover that this side of my family was unusual and bohemian. However, I thought to myself then that behind my natural father's unconventional and bohemian exterior was what I perceived to be a mental disorder which I found very disturbing. He was a man who lived in extreme isolation from the outside world and had completely given up taking care of himself, so I was shocked by his appearance and the surroundings in which he lived.

However, in the years that followed, I came to see that despite my natural father's quirks and oddities, he was an extraordinarily gifted thinker, artist and mathematician. In many ways he reminded me of pictures I had seen of the Russian mystic Rasputin, with his long unwashed hair, and his ragged clothes. His beard was long and wispy, like the wild and windswept marram grass. However, his ability to communicate was not good. He seemed quite unable to grasp that other people would not be so deeply interested in his special interests. This caused us both great frustrations.

As a result of meeting my natural father, I was to discover that I had other brothers and sisters I had known nothing about until then, including another son of his, my half-brother about fifteen years younger than me, whom I gradually got to know. At about the same time, I traced my natural mother too. I discovered that she went on to marry again and had other children, whom I have been able to meet on occasions. I feel very fortunate to have so many wonderful brothers and sisters from my natural parents.

Station 6
TENDERNESS

Jesus. There comes a time when words fail and only touch can bring your presence home. I feel so cut off from my body. I ache to feel the unity of my mind and body. My soul cries out for tenderness.

THE EXPERIENCE OF psychotherapy enabled me to develop self-awareness, empathy and compassion, which helped me to understand the ideas of reciprocity and forgiveness which had been alien concepts before. I found my anger's rightful home; I continued to grieve my losses and found new ways of expressing myself.

After years of struggle with anxiety and dissociative disorders, my body was aching for a way of being in the world where it would not be so compromised. It was because of all these difficulties that I became attracted to the Alexander technique.

The Alexander technique was founded by Fredrick Matthias Alexander, who was an Australian actor born in 1869 in Tasmania. While performing on stage he kept losing his voice. He received little help for his condition from his doctors, so he set himself the task of observing his posture with the use of mirrors, while reciting as though he was on stage. As a direct result of these observations, he was not only able to regain the use of his voice, but was able to pinpoint certain universal patterns of poor coordination which had caused him to lose his voice. From further observation of other people, he went on to brilliantly devise a practical and pragmatic approach to releasing tension throughout the whole body.

However, what fascinated me was that this way of observing and correcting ourselves was completely unlike all other relaxation techniques, in that at the core of its teaching was a way of breaking free of our habitual reaction to stimuli, and learning a new approach to life by applying the Alexander technique principles of constructive conscious control.

I found that this was just what I wanted, for I ached to be able to move beyond just reacting to life. I intuitively knew I had a gift for not reacting externally, and felt at home within the pragmatic, detached and at the same time contemplative dimensions that underpinned the work, for it seemed strangely natural to me. So, in the summer of 1994 I made the decision to train to be a teacher of the Alexander technique.

The great and mysterious incongruity of my emotional state, and the way it appeared not to press upon me, has always baffled me and others, so when I started the Alexander technique teacher-training course, I was able to 'hide naturally' my anxieties at being in such intense social contact. However, because of the very formalised and structured approach to touch, I was able to learn invaluable tools regarding touch and social contact, which had previously been an enigma to me.

Alexander work was invaluable in helping me restore my body and posture from the ravages of a lifetime of stress. It transformed my skeleton from one which was collapsed and bowed under the weight of enormous muscular tension, to one in which my spine and posture were more naturally aligned. However, at the same time as the Alexander technique was helping me to release into life, I was also unconsciously using the Alexander principles to conceal at greater depth my expressions of anxiety concerning sensory and social difficulties. So although the work clearly gave me enormous benefits, I was also able to find even more ways of acting 'normal' or unaffected. Another persona.

O how I longed to be more at home in my bones and my being in the presence of another.

Station 7
FALLING AGAIN

*Jesus. My survival skills, learned in adversity, are merely
taking me to a well that I cannot drink from. I am in a
world that at times seems not my own. How many falls
will it take until I can really stand in my truth?*

I AM FALLING AGAIN, for it seems that the world I had created and adapted for myself was one that had clearly passed its 'sell-by' date for me. My adapted self, although protecting me, was at the same time preventing me from moving on. This was a time which was as deeply interesting for me as it was terrifying, because the protective layers I had built up over the years were falling away and I was being exposed for the first time. I felt totally out of control over what was happening. It took me back to my early experiences when I was so afraid of going mad. The poet Yeats sums up my experience in 'The Second Coming', when he says 'Things fall apart; the centre cannot hold', and then in the last line from 'Easter 1916' he ends with 'A terrible beauty is born.'

At times the world did seem so intensely beautiful to me. The process of discovering myself was opening up a whole new world before my very eyes. It seemed that it was not so much my way of looking at the world that had changed, but that a whole landscape itself had been transformed. There is only one piece of poetry that can truly bring alive this chapter of my life. It is in the final scene of the film *American Beauty* directed by Sam Mendes. Kevin Spacey, who plays the part of Lester Burnham, a man whose life and marriage is falling apart, says,

I guess I could have been pretty pissed off with what had happened to me, but it's hard to stay mad when there's so much beauty in the world. Sometimes I feel like I am seeing it all at once and it's too much. My heart fills up like a balloon that's about to burst. And then I remember to relax and stop trying to hold on to it, and then it flows through me like rain and I can't feel anything but gratitude for every single moment of my stupid little life.

As well as continuing to receive one-to-one lessons with an Alexander teacher, I was also starting to attend self-help support groups for people with low self-worth and co-dependency issues. I found these meetings very helpful in being able to connect with other people, and to see that I was not the only person on the planet having problems with relationships and intimacy.

A sacred rule underpinning these groups was that there was to be no cross-talking while a member was expressing their thoughts and feelings. This was sacred for me indeed, because, for the first time in my life, it offered me a space that was mine, in order to express myself in the company of others. The cross-talking in other groups, or social situations, made it almost impossible for me to process my thoughts sufficiently to articulate the simplest of sentences.

I would very rarely socialise outside of the meetings, because I found from bitter experience that the 'no cross-talk rule' just went out of the window when people talked afterwards or went to the café. I also loved the way the meetings started and ended at exactly the same time each week. When the meetings ended, I just went home. I did not like the feeling of having to negotiate after-meeting talk. Don't get me wrong, I could do it, but it meant putting a face on again. I was also very susceptible to being flooded by people telling me their concerns because of my contemplative exterior and, besides that, because I find it so difficult to express my needs when someone is speaking fast, or constantly moving or waving their hands about. In the company of such people, I would often feel used up, and get stuck like a computer 'freezing'. Even though there was the support and comfort of the no cross-talk rule, I still had to program myself in order to express my thoughts and feelings within the four minutes we were allowed. For example, several days before the meetings I would systematically write down what my thoughts and feelings were and learn them by rote, regardless of whether or not I had moved beyond those very feelings by the time I got to the meeting.

If I did not have time to learn my feelings by rote, I would write them on my hand in shorthand, with very clear bullet points, so when it was my turn to share my thoughts and feelings, I would covertly look at the inside of my palm for my script, and at times jokes would be part of my repertoire too. It was like system-atically printing out a sentence in my mind, and then pressing a 'send' button which would allow words to come out. In a group situation, this is the only way I can ever participate, because the stimulation of being around others in a group floods my brain.

I credit these groups with giving me immense con-fidence, as for the first time in my life, I felt a part of a group, even if that group was highly structured and lasted only an hour and a half.

Station 8

WOMEN

Jesus. I see you surrounded by a determined procession of women. I, too, am surrounded here in this high-security military compound. Dogs with sabre-like teeth stare at me with their hungry eyes. High security fences with barbed wire reach to the sky. I ask you, how can I sustain my commitment to non-violence in a world that is so intent upon the use of force, condemnation and indifference to all that is of your way?

As a child, living at home had been like living in a war zone. A field of battle is a field of battle, and the need to disassociate, to split off from the imminent reality of death, is of equal importance in conventional warfare as it is in families where there is significant neglect. I learned this well through the intense psychotherapeutic process I went through. As I mentioned earlier, I learned empathy from being able to move beyond the intellectualisation of my feelings, and into learning to feel the feelings through the shattering and yet transformative process of grieving. However, my earliest experience of empathy came from identifying with the suffering of our family dogs, because my daily humiliations were very similar to theirs. I disliked violence with such intensity. However, I could equally see the violence of privilege and inequality of power and how that got played out with all my family.

My mother was always overweight, which often resulted in her being daily 'put down' by my father. I saw how she was being subjected to mockery and fell very short of my father's high expectations. So although my mother did things to the dogs and to me which I thought were cruel, I could see she was mentally unbalanced and very much the underdog herself, and for this reason I had a great affinity with her, an affinity that surpassed all the pain.

I feel sure that it was being exposed to these early experiences that formed my love of the underdog, the poor, and the despised. As a man of thirty, I was now asking some big questions: Where is God in all of this? How can I integrate such strong political convictions with the rebirth of my interest in God? So after exploring Eastern paths and disciplines, which were so compatible with the principles underpinning the Alexander technique, I felt a 'great hunger'. I saw this 'great hunger' as a desire for God.

Having abandoned my Catholic faith many years before, one Sunday I walked into a Catholic church in Highgate and attended Sunday mass for the first time in over twenty years. It was the same church where my adoptive parents got married in the late fifties, and also where my natural mother married in the late sixties. Going to church on that Sunday afternoon felt like a true homecoming for me.

At this time I picked up a book that was to change the course of my life for ever. The book was *Government is Violence* by Leo Tolstoy. In it Tolstoy outlines his theory of Christian anarchism and describes how the Sermon on the Mount was so instrumental to him in forming his radical convictions. I was deeply drawn into this blend of radical politics and devout religious faith.

Tolstoy held up to the light an image of Christ as a man who held a pacifist orientation to violence and an anarchist orientation to power. This book did more than just intrigue me – it set my heart on fire. And when I contemplated the story of Christ taking on the Empire, simply dressed and riding on a donkey, armed with nothing but tenderness and love, I fell in love with Jesus.

On a sunny day on Hampstead Heath, while reading Peter Marshall's *A History of Anarchism*, I came to the section on religious anarchism. It was here that I read about the Catholic Worker movement and its founders Dorothy Day and Peter Maurin. Inspired by what I had read about the Catholic Workers' strong passion for social justice and their deep commitment to the poor and marginalised, ideals which I also shared, I went into the Pax Christi office off the Holloway Road to find out if there were any contacts for the Catholic Worker movement in London. I spoke with the general secretary Pat Gaffney who informed me that there were no London contacts, but Pat told me that something interesting was happening in Liverpool that might interest me. I was given the telephone number of a man called Ciaron O'Reilly. The next week I was on a train heading north to Liverpool.

Ciaron O'Reilly had come over from Australia to support the four 'Seeds of Hope' Ploughshares activists. All four were dedicated women peace activists, inspired by the vision of Isaiah and Micah to 'beat swords into ploughshares' and were on trial in Liverpool for their disarmament action on the Hawk jets that were on their way to Indonesia, for the war on the people of East Timor.

It was a true baptism of fire for me to be among these religious peace activists who, like me, held such radical and prophetic convictions.

The steadfast commitment of many in the Catholic Worker movement to upholding this life ethic would lead us all that weekend to a high-security military compound in Preston, where the local parish priest, three refugees from East Timor and others were arrested for their actions.

I spent the whole of that Easter weekend in the community that Ciaron had brought together, in a large Catholic church on the outskirts of Liverpool city centre. We didn't know it at the time, but that weekend the Liverpool Catholic Worker movement was being infiltrated by intelligence agents working on behalf of British Aerospace. The news of the infiltration was broken by the *Observer* newspaper and it ran a story on the events of that whole weekend. Full transcripts of the intelligence reports were produced as the spies were uncovered. It made interesting reading – clearly the activities of the Catholic Worker movement were seen as posing a threat to the state. On the train home from Liverpool that weekend I pondered very deeply why more Christians weren't equally committed to peace and justice. Were we really so wrong in what we were doing in Liverpool?

Station 9

THE THIRD FALL

Jesus. All my life I have ached for what I have been unable to bear. Love. To be touched deeply by another. Here I am, completely drained of strength, trying to survive in this family.

THE SUMMER OF 1997 WAS without doubt the most exciting time of my life up till then, but it was also a crossroads in the sense that I had reached a point where I was wondering what direction my life should take next. I had just completed my Alexander technique training and had begun working as an Alexander technique teacher. It was a real gift to be able to work at long last, and to know I had a skill I was good at. The wonderful thing was that I realised I could truly shine and be totally present in myself with another person within the highly structured and time-disciplined environment that a one-to-one teaching session offered, in complete contrast to the difficulties I always experienced whenever I was in a group situation, when my calm and contemplative exterior concealed an inner turmoil. At last my quality of presence was the same on the inside as it appeared on the surface.

What a breakthrough, what wonderful opportunities I saw opening up for me! All I had ever wanted was to be able to own my gift and then to engage with the world using that gift. Exciting times indeed.

In addition, my contact with the Catholic Worker movement had revitalised my faith, a faith that in many ways had never disappeared, but was lying dormant, waiting to be set alight. I began to think long and hard about becoming a priest, so I started having preliminary talks with Father Pat, my local parish priest, who turned out to be one of the most gifted and generous priests I have ever met. As we got to know each other, he became a good friend to me and has remained so ever since.

But as things turned out, something happened which took my life in an unexpected direction.

One Saturday night, rather than spending the time on my own at home, I decided to go into Soho and walked into Bunjie's Coffee House. There was something about this folk and poetry scene that drew me in that night. I loved the place and was really taken by the friendly atmosphere there and in particular by the poetry and friendliness of Razz who ran the World Oyster Club there on Saturday nights. At the end of the night Razz came up to me and asked me to come back the next week and sing a couple of songs.

I had always seen life through the eyes of a poet, craving poetry from an early age as a means of expressing my connections to the world, and I had been writing songs for years. I had also taught myself to play the guitar after meeting my natural mother at her home, where she lived surrounded by guitars, and hearing her stories of how she had played with some of my favourite musicians. I had taught myself to play from old Donovan and Dylan sheet music, but was always keen to write my own songs and bring my poetry alive to music. Music also helped me to express my sadness and joy and it was therapeutic because the vibrations the sound produced were very calming when I played in the comfort of my own private space.

I had never performed my songs in front of others before, but I accepted Razz's invitation and turned up at Bunjie's the following week. In a sense I had been performing to people all my life, studying other people, observing how they interacted and reacted, how they laughed, how they showed their feelings and then trying to apply what I observed, coaching myself for the stage of life on which every step needed to be painstakingly planned, processed and executed. Driven by a great hunger and desire to learn to connect with other people, it had always taken hard work and persistence to 'learn my part' for any social situation – to do this I had to become a master craftsman in cutting and pasting my thoughts and reflections. Such means of expressing myself did enable me to get on in the world, and I found it a useful strategy in meetings. However, there were situations where a relationship needed to be conducted differently, when a 'cut-and-paste' approach didn't work, because it was detached, rehearsed and lacked spontaneity. I had already discovered that, in the world of intimate relationships, it was an ineffective form of communication, and I now discovered that it was also ineffective when performing in front of an audience. I soon realised that not only was I unable to sing and look at the audience at the same time, which I overcame by shutting my eyes completely in order to shield myself from the intensity of stimuli coming from the audience, but also I was unable to interact and converse with the audience in between songs because I had not prepared anything beforehand. The spontaneity shown by other singers was impossible for me, so I didn't speak at all, or just one or two sentences at the most, or a simple message, had to suffice.

Something else I had to miss out on was socialising at the end of the evenings at Bunjie's as this was too much for me. It took such skill for me to be able to get through one lot of socialising that I couldn't cope with more. So I always left early, a habit I rely upon, as I have very fixed routines towards bedtime.

However, I saw my difficulties with interaction as a great challenge. After all, I had spent a lifetime of having no friends and no social life, now at least I was getting opportunities of meeting interesting and creative people. This was in itself way beyond my wildest dreams as a child and when in hospital. It never ceased to amaze me that I was out there, engaging with people, making friends, performing to them. I hadn't really lived, loved or touched people until then, but now what was unfolding for me was work, social life, the Catholic Worker movement and music and the folk scene. I suppose this was a honeymoon period in my life – I was young, free and meeting people on my terms. I was convinced that if I devoted more time to the process of psychotherapy and self-help meetings, I would find I could overcome my difficulties and find greater freedom of expression and love. I really believed that I was just two or three steps or a few more primal episodes away from lasting happiness – if I kicked and screamed a few more times I would be free.

Then something happened which changed my life for ever. One day Razz fell ill and he asked me to do his full set. I was very pleased to fill in for him. It just so happened that there was a woman in the audience who caught my attention. She seemed to have all the qualities which I found most attractive in women – gentleness and sensitivity, combined with some kind of counter-cultural difference. Conventional women held very little allure for me, whereas women who were different, without trying to be, held enormous appeal for me. Although I was not very skilled in managing myself in relationships, I had had three or four relationships with women in the past, but when I met Sarah and began to get to know her, I had never felt so excited. Not only was she attractive, quiet, gentle and thoughtful, she was also a Christian. I really looked forward to spending time with her, though there was a fair bit of anxiety mixed with the excitement. She lived outside London so I used to travel over to see her most weekends, but on the journey back home I felt very lonely and unsettled.

After I had known her for a year, I had given up all thoughts of the priesthood and made up my mind that

I wanted to marry her. So I made one of the biggest decisions of my life – to move out of London to be with Sarah and her two children.

Within a couple of weeks I was having panic attacks and felt emotionally and physically exhausted. I found the constant noise of children, televisions and general social interaction left me feeling disorientated, as if I was living in a kaleidoscope of colour amidst a carousel that never stopped moving. People, places and things just seemed to flood into me. I felt totally overwhelmed.

The enormity of change was too much for me to bear. My thinking became very obsessive-compulsive, and I was starting to check and re-check things like electricity switches, locks and doors and things of value and importance, like keys and my wallet. I also started having awful intrusive thoughts. But I was unable to convey to Sarah the level of distress I felt. I was deeply ashamed of my inability to manage myself well regarding the anxiety associated with her children, and felt very alone. I felt truly lost in this family which had opened their hearts and their home to me.

Station 10
BEING STRIPPED

Jesus. My little Daniel has taken me out of my place of hiding and into a world I am barely able to survive in. His tenderness strikes me to the core. I can no longer comfortably wear my 'cloak of evasion'. I feel humiliated, yet even in my nakedness, my true self remains deeply concealed.

IF THERE WAS ONE EVENT that I had to pick out in my life that I treasured above all else, it would be the birth of my son. I cannot really come close to explaining quite how I felt on the day I saw him come into the world, but the overriding feeling was one of excitement. The whole family had been in a state of increasing excitement in the weeks leading up to the birth. In spite of the anxiety I had concerning the problems between myself and Sarah, the impending birth had brought the whole family closer together. People say the birth of their child is the most wonderful moment in their lives and it certainly was for me, and will remain so. The labour had seemed long and distressing and I was so relieved when it was over. I was so overjoyed when I finally held him in my arms. None of us knew whether it would be a boy or a girl and I was delighted it was a boy. We called him Daniel. It was wonderful introducing him to the rest of the family – to his brother and sister first, then, within the next few days, to his grandparents and aunt. And the house was a sea of cards.

But the excitement lasted for only a few days before there came a dramatic shift from all the fun and excitement to all the problems. I loved him intensely, but Daniel's arrival had thrown my closely regulated lifestyle into chaos. I had already struggled with the noise and demands of the older children, but the noise and demands of a newborn baby were far greater, and this, when combined with a lack of sleep, soon became unbearable for me.

I loved to hold him with great tenderness, but it always seemed to me that the other members of the family would love and tend him in ways which seemed more natural than I could be. It was as though all the naturalness, 'tendedness' and 'tended-to-ness' all around me highlighted my own unnaturalness and extreme awkwardness. I felt ashamed that I couldn't 'work it', couldn't be natural, and because I felt I wasn't good enough, I felt I needed to try harder. I thought I should be doing more and that I shouldn't complain. I became afraid that I would be seen as inferior and redundant, so I became jealous of his brother and sister.

I also became paranoid that someone would steal my son from me, and that I would lose him as I had lost my natural mother when I was the same age as him. The bond I felt with Daniel was very special, and I had always lost things that were special to me.

The stress of this constant and unrelenting anxiety played itself out in many ways. I did not have an open and honest relationship with the older children, so I couldn't explain to them why I became very possessive of Daniel and wouldn't let them pick him up or hold him. As a result, my relationship with the other children deteriorated as they found my over-protectiveness understandably oppressive and uncomfortable to live with.

After four months, with my internal coping strategies completely shattered, I climbed out of the upstairs window and wandered off into the night. Although I returned a couple of weeks later, I felt unable to live in the family home, and found a flat in town.

I walked out of a family and into a very adult drama of managing parental responsibilities amidst the pain of separation. I felt angry and misunderstood. I felt broken-hearted to have lost everything I had longed for, for so long, and experienced the strange calm that only comes when one has nothing left to lose. I remained living in the same area for a couple of years and I would see Daniel every week. This was a lonely time for me, but it must also have been so difficult for Sarah and her other two children as well.

I continued offering the Alexander technique during this time, despite the enormous stress I was under. I started to reflect on the contemplative dimension of Alexander work, and how it offered me a way of being free and 'being' this freedom in the presence of another person, even if this freedom was still only to be found within the formalised structure of the Alexander lesson. I was also starting to see how my work could help in meditation and began developing an interest in the Christian contemplative tradition.

Often in my weekly time with Daniel, I would take him to his playgroup, and it was here that I really had to work hard at concealing my distress, as I found being around lots of children took me back to my own childhood. I felt flooded by all the sensory stimulation and interaction with mothers and their children and had the urge to bite myself and make lots of comforting noises to help me vent the enormous level of stress that built up inside me.

I returned to London in 2003 and after establishing a good working relationship with Sarah I continued to be able to visit Daniel every fortnight and speak with him most days on the phone.

Dorothy Day, of the Catholic Worker movement, loved quoting Dostoyevsky, 'Love in action is a harsh and dreadful thing compared with love in dreams.' My experience of trying so hard to love my son at the same time as coping with all the difficulties surrounding this, has, I feel, taken me into the deepest meaning behind these words.

Station 11

CRUCIFIXION

*Jesus. To bear the beams of Daniel's love feels, at times,
like nails being driven into my very being. The weight of
the world seems truly upon my shoulders. Why am I the
way I am?*

Love, closeness and feelings of deep intimacy and communion with another, can flood me with an overwhelming sense of sensation. Being physically touched by another is not one of my issues now as an adult; however, being touched deeply internally is. My usual way of coping, whenever situations became too difficult for me, had always been to walk quietly away, but for the first time in my life I found myself in a painful situation I couldn't walk away from. Because I felt such great love for Daniel, this time I couldn't pull back and turn away – I was 'nailed' and couldn't break away. What was worse, although I loved him more than anything else in the world, the deep feeling of at-oneness whilst being in his company caused such awful intrusive thoughts and awkwardness, it felt like some strange kind of 'empathic backlash' and as such, it felt as if nails were being driven into my very being. It would be understandable to see such difficulties purely in the context of Daniel's innocence and tenderness unlocking my vulnerability, my resistance to this experience of intimacy coming in the form of these awful thoughts when I was spending time with him and when we were playing together. However, after all my years of psychotherapy, something still seemed terribly amiss which I couldn't account for. This mystery was killing me. It felt as if I was being crucified.

My whole life has been a struggle to reconcile seemingly irreconcilable opposites. Whether those opposites are within me or in political or philosophical ideas, I feel drawn and compelled to see the complementarity and the unity in everything I see. Often I would reflect on Christ's Sermon on the Mount and what I believed was the central message of this radical sermon, which is to love our enemies. I often reflected that if I were able to love my enemies, then I would have no enemies, but that the process of forgiving has to move from the heart and not the head, that is, if it is organic and not superimposed by outside influences through fear, coercion or scrupulosity. Can we really give to another that which we have yet to integrate in ourselves – peace?

To be a follower of Jesus, I have always seen it as a personal challenge for me to 'learn to bear the beams of love', as William Blake said.

Just as Simon Peter reacted in horror when Jesus attempted to wash his feet, Jesus' response to Simon Peter was that if he wanted to follow him, he had to learn to bear the pain of too much tenderness.

There is something about receiving that is so much harder than giving. And now because of my circumstances in having to travel far from my home and my fixed routines on my fortnightly visits to Daniel, I was in real need of receiving help and support from others. Friendship for me now took on a new dimension, because it is one thing to pay a therapist or to go to a support group for help, but it is quite another thing to ask for help from a friend. Up to now I had been independent, with a great investment in that independence. Now I was doing the one thing I had never done in my life – ask for help. This was something I was not comfortable doing and it took me some time to get used to it.

I am flooded with gratitude to those dear friends who helped me after my separation from Sarah – they were like Good Samaritans to me. Among these were Marek and Maria who opened their hearts and their home to me each time I visited Daniel, and they have continued to do so. There was also Katherine, who became like the mother I never had, and her daughter Alison who, like her mother, would patiently 'listen with love' to my difficulties. I couldn't have managed without them all – their help with 'bearing my beams' was invaluable.

And then there was Patrick, a Benedictine monk who had just come out from the monastery to live the life of Julian of Norwich.

I met Patrick in a little chapel, where, just like the fourteenth-century anchoress before him, he sat in prayerful silence, and engaged with anyone who expressed an interest in the spiritual life, be they tourist, pilgrim, or just curious of his presence.

I approached him and asked if I could learn the art of contemplation from him. For some time I had been helping people see how the Alexander technique can facilitate in taking the fruits of contemplation into everyday life experiences. In order to deepen these skills of discernment and mindfulness, I was eager to learn more about contemplative practice and meditation.

His advice was to give up all desire of 'doing' anything. This was a great disappointment to me at the time, yet as our relationship grew, I came to see that the solitary life was familiar to me, and Patrick viewed the world in very similar ways to myself. We both felt the need to escape. In the same way that a prisoner of war saw it as his natural duty to escape the prison, we were united in our call to escape the prison of the world.

The attraction to the solitary life and the life of the anchorite became deeply appealing. The love that Patrick showed me was deeply affirmed in the twice-weekly meetings we had, spanning an eighteen-month period. I was listened to with such tenderness and love, that it left me in no doubt whatsoever where my true vocation lay.

So in 2006, I too began to train for such a vocation at the very same place where he learned his craft, so that I could learn the more structured skills of a spiritual director. The course was held just one evening a week, and because I received a lot of support from the tutors and other members of the group, my anxieties that I would find the course too difficult were allayed. It was a gentle, caring, non-competitive environment, otherwise I couldn't have done it.

In the meantime, my priority was Daniel and all my energy and meagre resources would be devoted to loving him. However, it was my anxiety over being with him that was the constant struggle which weighed me down.

Station 12

DEATH

Jesus. For me, true prayer and love can only ever really be learned in the hour when prayer becomes impossible and my heart turns to stone. I so wish this was not so — but it is the way I am.

I FELT I HAD DIED INSIDE. For not being able to name my struggle was starting to cause me immense distress. After thirteen years of recovery and therapy, why was I again depressed, why was I unable to sustain healthy loving relationships, why was I unable to find sustainable employment and most importantly of all, WHY, WHEN TAKEN OUT OF MY ROUTINES WHILST BEING WITH MY SON, DID I EXPERIENCE THIS STRANGE DISABLING ANXIETY IN HIS COMPANY? I felt redundant at the core of my being.

At night when I would put Daniel to bed, we would recall the day's events, and reflect upon the time during the day when we felt happy and sad. We would give thanks for the happy times and ask God for help in those moments that were painful or difficult.

An avid football fan, Daniel's high points were always scoring one goal or another or making a spectacular save. Very rarely did he express a sad moment, apart from a Tottenham defeat or an Arsenal victory! His high points in the day were most likely mine also. What pleasure it gave me to see him so wild and joyful. However, how could I start to explain that such joyful and spontaneous experiences would not only take me out of my routine way of being in the world, but would often be followed by awful intrusive thoughts and anxiety? How could I say, at this special time, that my best times were my worst times? Not knowing why this was, made life unbearable and unendurable.

I started to contemplate thoughts of suicide, but such thoughts revolted me. For most of my adult life I have always thought of suicide as a permanent solution to a temporary problem, but now I was struggling to sustain my faith and my life. I had two terribly addictive and painful relationships at this time, which I saw solely in the context of acting out my traumatic past. These experiences just reinforced my sense of hopelessness and subsequently resulted in me joining yet another support group.

Station 13

LAMENTATION

*Jesus. The weight of the world no longer seems so press-
ing upon my shoulders. My mind, my body and soul
offer little resistance. I have nothing left.*

STILL UNABLE TO MAKE any sense of what was wrong in my life, I started to feel a sense of defeat that was increasingly gathering pace and consuming me. I felt straitjacketed within myself. I started to lose all hope of ever being a true part of the world around me. I felt a crushing sadness that for most of my time with Daniel I felt horribly crippled inside and frequently whilst being with him would cry inwardly with despair. My throat would feel swollen with tension, such was the extent to which I would forcibly swallow down my sadness.

I would be mentally shattered by the time I boarded my train home to London after my time with Daniel. It was here on these fortnightly journeys back to the capital, whilst looking out of the train window, that for the first time in my life I felt such intense relief and release of tension at the prospect of death.

I was starting to isolate myself from my friends, and spent a lot of time on my own in Highgate cemetery writing poetry. I found deep solace here amongst the gravestones and sculptures and wildlife in this beautiful place. My favourite time of day was always after closing time, when the keeper locked the gates; I used to climb through the gap in the old rusty fence. I felt safe here. I watched the sunset and I communed with the foxes, finches and wild cats.

I knew I was clinically depressed, but the greater concern for me was my inability in expressing the intensity of pain I was in. I felt like that wooden scarecrow in the playground of my childhood. It was this agony that led me to buy a packet of razor blades on my way home from Highgate one night. I ached to visualise the horror of my despair, to get it out in the open. I was unable to articulate what was at the root of the problem. So, although my friends knew I was very depressed, their words of support were no longer reaching me.

When I got home, I sat on the floor of my lounge and opened one of the blades from its wrapping. My hands were trembling. It is true that I had drunk large amounts of alcohol prior to getting home. However, deep inside me, I felt strangely focused and calm about what I was about to do. The first cut produced an explosion of blood and made my whole body shudder. The speed at which the blood flowed from me shocked me at first, but then I felt the most enormous relief that is beyond expression.

I felt an opium-like effect flood my whole body and my whole being. I no longer felt fearful or anxious, or even depressed for that matter. Watching the blood forming into various pools on my white vinyl flooring was striking but not disturbing. The disturbing thing was not being able to get my pain out into the world. Now it was spilling out of me for the world to see. I cut myself like this three or four times that evening, and repeated this ritual for five nights running.

Never in my life had I done such things to myself, and yet through this bloodletting I felt real for the first time in my life. Real, in that I was no longer a scarecrow, but a human being visually expressive and able for the first time in my life to externalise the internal distress, through neither poetry nor intellectual articulation, but through physical expression. It brought relief from the pain I was in. However, the lacerations on my arms were so bold and striking that they unsettled me.

I went to visit my friend Razz in Tottenham. It was a beautiful summer's day and I was buying some groceries from a shop in the High Street. While I was queuing up to pay, I saw a little girl of about six staring at the lacerations on my arms. The little girl then gently walked over to me and said, 'Excuse me, sir. Do you fight tigers?' 'No, sweetie,' I said. But I wanted to say to her, 'But I do fight demons.' I left the shop deeply affected by this experience.

Then it was Daniel's seventh birthday, and I was invited to his party. It was a beautiful midsummer's day and I was severely depressed. When people started playing pass the parcel, I went over the road to hide in the caravan I used when I was visiting. But soon there was a knock at the door of the caravan. It was Daniel's sister, informing me that he was cutting the cake. I was so thankful for her doing this; I often felt that she had something of an understanding of my problems. I ached to be there for Daniel, but I felt like an alien, an imprisoned spectator.

Doing normal things normally is an alien concept for me. Of course externally, due to my ability to simulate normality, I appear very normal, but inside I can be totally lost, confused and overwhelmed. While the children were running around in the garden in the hot sunshine, I was trying so hard to conceal the scars on my arms, which were the only outward signs that all was not well within.

Overwhelmed by my inability to join in the fun, I was thinking of hiding out in the caravan again, when I saw a little boy who seemed so lost. He stuck out because he did not know how to play with the others. I asked him if he wanted to play with me. He said, 'Yes.' I was deeply relieved, and so too was he. So the two of us played in our own little world. We felt safe, enjoyed each other's company and I felt I could breathe somewhat.

My journey home to London after the party was a long one. I felt convinced that I was totally incompetent and useless as a father and that my son would be better off without a father who was so crippled.

Images of my natural father, and the little boy I played with at the party, constantly flashed in and out of my awareness. Because of the extreme mental distress I was in at the time, deep down I still felt that I had inherited something of my father's 'madness' that was incurable and now terminal. Also, the little boy at the party reminded me of the magic of finding a special friend, and transported me back to my child-hood and the constant references by my mother to my 'madness'. That I might really be mad was the thing that terrified me more than anything else.

Station 14

LAID TO REST

*Jesus. Have mercy on my soul. Please take care of my son
and his mother, sister and brother. I have no words left
and everything is silent, like snow falling upon snow.*

MY PRAYER LIFE entered into uncharted territory. Intellectually I always felt I knew what Thomas Merton once said: 'True prayer and love can only really be learnt in the hour when prayer becomes impossible and your heart turns to stone.' However, my prayer life was now fast moving away from all concepts and interesting quotations. Somehow there was real meaning to be found in remaining faithful in this time of overwhelming suffering. But now the only faith I had was with God, and God taking care of my soul after my death. I learnt at this time that it is not an absence of affliction or distraction that characterises a person of faith, but instead a deep desire to remain faithful when all seems lost. I felt ready to meet God.

Having been hospitalised for severe depression as an adolescent, I feel I have developed over the years a rather cautious and discerning attitude when using the language of the apophatic and contemplative, especially when conveying the interior movements of what I believe to be my soul in great anguish and suffering.

However, a state of complete and utter despair was soon to come upon me. My soul now in complete darkness, I contemplated suicide. I have no words to convey the horror that was now unfolding within me, acutely aware that the preparations I was now making would tear at the souls of those I love and open a wound so deep in Daniel, a wound that could never be fully healed in this life.

On my return to London, I started to plan for my suicide in great detail. I gathered all my favourite pictures of the two of us together, and put them in a big picture frame; the pictures were wet with the tears that fell. I hoped that Daniel would somehow be helped in forgiving me through seeing the stains my tears made on the pictures. Nothing at all was insulating me from the horror of where I was heading and what I would leave behind. My plan was to wait until after my next visit to Daniel, so that this way he would not associate his birthday with my death.

At this time I recall a psychotherapist friend asking me how my last visit to my son had gone. My reply was very strange indeed, for I said I felt like an autistic boy at a disco. In conversation later on, this same friend asked me if my natural father had any history of mental illness. I can recall feeling very threatened indeed by his prying questions. This leading question had its place in the context of a previous conversation earlier in the evening, when I had mentioned that when I was fifteen my adoptive parents, dismayed at my hospitalisation, wrote away to the Crusade of Rescue, enquiring whether there was any history of mental disorder in my natural parents.

I had been reading the lives of the saints, particularly that of St Theresa of Lisieux, whose faithfulness in her trials I found inspiring. So one night I got down on my knees and prayed to her to take my prayer to God and intervene in an attempt to avert the impending tragedy. I realised, while I was praying to St Theresa, the influence that years of good manners had had on my prayer life. In becoming aware of this, I was able to fully empty myself from the depths of my heart. I was then able to take my lifetime's anger, hopelessness and despair to God.

The extent of my depression seemed complete. I was spiritually and emotionally unable to face the despair of my inability to integrate into the world any longer.

The day after my prayer to St Theresa, I travelled once more to see my son. I was convinced this would be the last time I would see him. I spent the night with him in the caravan. I looked into his face that night when he fell asleep in my arms. I loved him so much, I would do anything for him, but now the pain was too great, too great to do the one thing he would be sure to want above all else, which was for me to stay alive. That night in the caravan my heart splintered into a thousand pieces. My soul was in such agony that there are no words to convey the depth of desolation I felt at the time. My head was full of demons screaming at me; my soul offered no resistance. I was taken over by death.

Having read and studied the poets and religious writers in my attempt to learn the language of desolation, I had come across the writings of Emile Durkheim, who was the founding father of modern sociology and author of *Suicide*, which has now become a classic and authoritative work, widely acknowledged as the most penetrating and insightful of any such study.

I had a burning desire to end my suffering in this life. However, equal to this was the desire to cause as little as possible ambiguity and confusion as to my motives. I felt that if this was understood, if somehow I was able to convey the horror of my trapped world, I would be forgiven, and thus those I loved would find freedom and acceptance of my action, and their resulting anger, resentment and grief would be softened.

On the train home I found myself engaging in an exercise I learned on my spiritual direction course, which involved the process of spontaneous drawing and discernment. I felt such deep relief to be away from the intensity of despair. I wrote on a big piece of paper, 'Where is God when I am with Daniel?' I sat in silence for a minute or two and then drew. What I drew changed my life, and what had somehow evaded me all my life was dramatically revealed to me in that moment.

What I drew revealed to me that I had autism.

The picture was of me with Daniel. I drew a stick man, representing myself, encircled by several lines which were symbolic of walls. My head was surrounded by circles too, next to which I wrote, 'Not a halo, but a loop of hell'. There were also speech bubbles coming out of my head with the caption, 'Help!' My little Daniel was drawn with his hands in the air, jumping for joy saying, 'Daddy, this is fun.' However, what was deeply revealing for me were the sharp lines that I drew radiating out from Daniel towards my heart. These lines I interpreted at first as sparks, and then it hit me that in fact they represented a force, and that this force radiating from Daniel was his beams of love for me. The flood of feeling from Daniel was like an assault which produces a profound emotional reaction in me, the intensity of which I am unable to express. So the 'loop of hell' was a neurological reaction to an empathic flow of energy.

Something in this drawing perhaps unconsciously reminded me of a drawing I had seen about a month earlier when I had visited an exhibition of art work by autistic people. This, combined with my thoughts about my natural father and about my 'madness', somehow made me come to this new realisation.

The next day I began looking up autism on the internet and got in touch with a psychologist who was affiliated to the National Autistic Society. My autism was finally confirmed ten days later, when I travelled to Lancashire for a formal diagnostic assessment with her.

I do believe that what happened was a miracle.

Using football analogy here, I felt I had not only

won the FA Cup Final, but saw with such clarity my struggles of the past, and how every day was like an away game. I felt vindicated and deeply affirmed in one fell swoop. This was a true awakening.

Station 15
RESURRECTION

*Jesus. I awake from darkness. The cloud of unknowing
lifts. So too does my depression, like the mist at the
dawn of a new day. I take my first gentle steps across
this bridge. The bridge that now leads from my true
and deepest self into the world.*

Awakenings can produce great elation as well as disorientation from seeing life in such a radically new way. Living life consciously for the first time as a man with autism was overwhelming in itself, especially as the diagnosis came right at the end of such a severe depression that my life was in danger. My whole orientation and view of myself and the world was now turned upside down and inside out.

The day I received my diagnosis I sent a text to my friends back home. It read:

> DIAGNOSED. Diagnosed as autistic as a child. Now as an adult diagnosed with Asperger's syndrome. Depression lifting like the mist at the dawn of a new day.

I will never forget the joy I felt in writing that text. The joy was simple. The joy was that Daniel would not have to face tragedy and insurmountable loss as a result of my suicide. A suicide that would have been irreversible had this cloud of unknowing not been lifted that day. This is neither exaggeration nor melodrama, just cold fact.

The greatest challenge in my life is to love my son, and to pass on to him something beautiful and life-affirming, so that he can be truly himself. I trust that, amidst the tragedies and unfairness of life, he will be able to never lose sight of the fact that the world is a beautiful place and that God is right in the centre of it all and that Daniel will be free to be himself.

Some weeks after receiving my diagnosis, I watched cine-film footage of my childhood. It was as if I were watching it with new eyes. Most clips were of me playing with my sister at seaside locations, or playing in the garden. As I watched myself mockingly grimacing (acting a feeling), and observed my body contorted and distorted by tension, I felt deep compassion for myself. Tears fell from my eyes, but these were not tears of sadness nor of loss, but tears of pure joy, the joy of finally coming home. I observed how my sister would have free range of facial expression, when, for example, she dived into the sea or swimming pool, whereas I would not express on the outside any reaction whatsoever.

It is fascinating now to see my face as a young child in this footage, for this enabled me to recall my thoughts and feelings at this particular time. Often my thoughts would have been something like, 'How do I pull the right face appropriate for this thought or feeling?' Even when in pain, say if I would stub my toe or have painful falls, it seemed mysterious to me how to convey feelings by physical expression. I understand now that it would have been a neurological impossibility.

As I grew up, what I had learned to do was to act. It was as if I was forever standing outside of myself and, like some mystical puppeteer, pulling strings connected to my facial features. Subsequently, acting became my 'normal'. Concealing my feelings so well by using imitation and acting to achieve superficial social competence, resulted inevitably in having considerable difficulty convincing people that I have real problems with social understanding and empathy. In both emotional and social situations I became too plausible in my role to be believed.

The diagnosis with Asperger's syndrome has reconciled seemingly irreconcilable opposites in me that had previously baffled psychologists and the many people who knew me. This story helps me to sit in that reconciliation and to journey deeper into the integration of my self and the world.

> I dreamt last night,
> O marvellous error,
> That there were honeybees in my heart,
> Making honey out of my old failures.
>
> Antonio Machado

In my introduction I referred to the words of Thomas Merton, 'To be a saint is to be truly oneself'. Living so painfully unaware of my autism, I had been so far removed from my deepest nature, which had shrouded and concealed something so fundamental as to who I am and have always been. Because of this new understanding of myself now, I feel confident that Daniel will not have to go through the distress of not knowing himself, particularly if he turns out to have inherited any autistic traits from me. His is undoubtedly a deeply sensitive, thoughtful and beautiful soul.

I feel that for a child to be able to be themselves, it is of great importance for the parents to be themselves too. In this respect I feel a great sense of happiness for us both, that our time together from now on will be strengthened and hope-filled as a result of knowing myself better, as is already proving to be the case.

I have a little caravan in the woods near to where Daniel lives. It is here that we play and eat together. It is here that I sleep each fortnight and it is here that he runs in the morning, to jump into my sleeping bag and wriggle close to me to keep warm. It is in these moments that it becomes clear to me that it is my son who has taken me out of my comfort zone and into the world. Just as Jesus said, 'A little child shall lead them', sure enough it was Daniel who has led me into tenderness and love, and thus my very new understanding of myself as a man with autism. Just as Jesus called forth Lazarus from the tomb, Daniel has brought me into the light of day.

IN CONCLUSION

As the mist continues to lift, it reveals a bridge. This bridge seems to be the means whereby I can now walk from my hidden inner world into the world at large. The scars on my arms I now see as midwifery marks that facilitated this painful birthing/joyful event. Like many painful labours, I needed medical and medicinal support to pull through and take my first steps across that bridge.

Coming off my anti-depressants gave me the freedom to feel. No longer insulated by the emotional blunting the medication offered, I live now a free man, free to feel the enormity of this story.

The missing piece of the jigsaw, my autism, the essential part of my deepest self, has finally been found, and part of putting it into place is writing this story and sharing it with friends. It is one thing to write a story like this, and quite another thing to sit and breathe through it all. For this reason I am very fortunate indeed to have made good friends on the journey, where I can be listened to with gentleness and love, and thus helped in bringing my story home.

Concealing my difference makes me ill, and being my difference sets me free. This is the conclusion many of us in the autistic spectrum come to sooner or later. It has taken me forty-two years to understand this fully.

My post-diagnosis counselling has made this abundantly clear.

Within weeks of my diagnosis I was introduced by a friend to a woman from New York called Franny who had worked for many years as a behavioural consultant to people with autism in America. She made me see how I had 'severed' my autistic hands for reasons of survival and that, as a result, I had suffered from depression for many years.

During the four meetings I had with Franny, she taught me many things. She taught me all about de-compromising strategies, and the importance of utilising them in order to dampen down the hyper-arousal of my nervous system. She helped me see that by abandoning my natural ways of surviving in an overwhelming world I had lost my 'wings', and thus my natural way of being in this world, a world in which I was dying, in my attempts to conform and unconsciously conceal my autism.

She understood all my problems with sensory issues and need for space, and at last I felt deeply understood regarding the anxiety I had around creative play and the very complex difficulties I had whilst being with Daniel. Franny also taught me that the autistic brain has no filter and therefore everything floods in and people with autism can become drowned in information. This explains perfectly all my learning and processing difficulties. So she taught me practical ways of reducing over-stimulation from my environment, both within my home and outside. These included decorating my rooms in calm colours, changing my diet to eliminate foods which might contribute to stress, reducing stress from light and sound when I was out by wearing sunglasses and earplugs, and ways of bringing me back into myself when in stressful or over-stimulating situations, for example, by squeezing my arm, which has a remarkably calming effect on the nervous system.

Franny taught me how to be happy as a man with autism, and that autism is a gift, but a gift which needs to be cared for. I learned that routines, one of the many autistic traits I have felt so ashamed about, contain and hold this gift. With such awareness comes the good fortune of choice – to be my difference or to conceal my difference. One leads to the light and the other to where I was clearly languishing.

Apart from Franny's help, information on the internet has been invaluable for learning as much as I could about autism and Asperger's syndrome. Details of some of these sites have been listed at the end of the book. With the knowledge gained here I have been able to make sense of many things in my life which have always been difficult for me to understand, including showing emotion by appropriate facial expression, as I referred to earlier, and also eye contact.

Many people with Asperger's syndrome have difficulty with eye contact, as I can when tired and unable to control my anxieties from manifesting themselves. People have told me that my ability to give eye contact is very good. Most times when not tired, I am able to neither stare nor constantly wander off centre. However, my ability to focus on the minute details of something at the expense of the whole picture is, as with many people in the autistic spectrum, a gifted skill. Seeing life through the eyes of a contemplative, my focusing away the glare of the other is complete. Like the innermost centre of a hurricane, there is stillness and beauty. It is here in the essence of the other I can actually find rest, experience wonder and see Christ mirrored. However, when tired, like magic, this lovely experience evades me and my eyes can burn with pain from the strain of it all. Also, this gift, unusual for a person with Asperger's syndrome, is equally ineffective if the other is constantly moving, making a noise or is agitated.

Explaining these things is important for me because not having a physical disability which can be seen leaves me open to being misunderstood. In my case, I have been told that I have an extraordinary and highly advanced set of adaptive skills formed out of emotional and brutal necessity.

Without doubt, these highly advanced adapted skills, born out of adversity and refined through psycho-therapy, self-help groups, as well as the Alexander technique, all proved invaluable to my being able to express myself on many levels. However, these gifts of self-awareness proved totally redundant in bringing to light my autism and thus the underlying distress of managing myself with Daniel. Those lines from William Blake, which I have already quoted in the introduction and referred to in Station 11, say it so well:

... We are put on earth a little space
That we may learn to bear the beams of love.

On that memorable train ride home from visiting
Daniel, it was the picture of his 'beams of love' that
penetrated deep into my inner world with all its neurological complexities. It is now well understood that the
power of spontaneous drawing can override our left-
brain dominance, which is more rational and analytical,
and put us more in touch with the intuitive and creative
parts of ourselves.

The empathic response of people with autism is very
different from the neurologically typical person.
Psychologists specialising in autism call this difference
'Theory of Mind', which simply means the impaired
ability to recognise and understand thoughts, beliefs,
desires and intentions of other people, in order to make
sense of their behaviour. However, there are autistics
like me who are extremely oversensitive to the feelings
of others as opposed to being immune to them, but who
cannot handle the painful feedback this initiates for
them. This explains wonderfully and demystifies completely my complicated anxiety, as well as entering into
the essence of how I interpret Blake's 'beams of love'
quotation.

It seems that this particular oversensitive autistic
patterning has much in common with my ability to
attune myself to others, another painful gift I possess.
However, this gift was born out of necessity in childhood in order to attune myself to my mother's needs, as

a result of my mother's inability to attune herself to mine. So what I lack with regard to a natural empathic response, I overcompensate for with my advanced skills of emotional and cognitive empathy refined through adversity and the hard painful work I have done on myself over many years.

A useful image here would be that of a water pump, for while the average person has a natural and effortless supply of empathy, I, on the other hand, would have to work this system manually and with great effort. As my emotional routing is well used, I have now developed a capacity to empathise, but it is from the well of emotion and experienced feelings. Here psychotherapy has been invaluable, in offering me a link to the world of others. By learning to feel my feelings, not just objectifying them and rationalising them, I was able to link to the feelings of others, but this was not always so. When I was younger I could never imagine what effect my actions might have on someone else, for example, when taking part in the offences which led to my criminal record. This was a totally alien concept for me then, that my actions might be hurting someone. As it was, I ended up with a criminal record, which although for a crime considered to be a juvenile offence, and subsequently a spent conviction, would be a record for life and hinder me in my attempts to find work.

It stills remains the case that there are some people in the medical world who remain convinced that it is impossible for people with Asperger's syndrome to communicate at depth or love another person because of our empathic complexities. I am living proof that this is not true, for I fit comfortably within the autistic spectrum, sufficiently to qualify as having Asperger's syndrome as defined and outlined by the Autism Diagnostic Interview (ASDI-R) diagnostic criteria.

Just because many people with autism, like myself, are undeniably self-centred, this does not mean we are necessarily selfish. It is true that perhaps we live in our own world, but it is a world within THE world. Natural empathy is a sense, not a virtue, and because we can lack this natural response, we generally overcompensate in other areas and often this forces us down into hidden depths in order to connect with others. Applying this to myself, for example, when offering spiritual direction or the Alexander technique, I feel totally attuned at depth to others. This is simply due to the contemplative conditions inherent in both disciplines, which create the conditions that could never be experienced in the multi-stimuli environment of the group. Consequently my 'cut and paste' strategies become wonderfully redundant, and I can feel the spirit moving within me.

I BEGAN MY INTRODUCTION with the quotation

'Your joy is your sorrow unmasked'.

As my sorrowful mask of normality is being shed, I can see now how other people's normality was my path to insanity and suicide.

My diagnosis with Asperger's syndrome has helped me to see that because of my childhood trauma, all my life I have unconsciously associated my unusual ways with being mad or insane. In being able to own my mask of normality, with all its neurological components, I have been able to start integrating, and thus befriending, that part of me that has forever been unacceptable. Making peace with our 'shadow' is holy work indeed.

I feel deeply that great parallels can be drawn here with the contemplative path and Jungian psychology, working with the 'shadow', or the parts of ourselves which we deem unacceptable or challenging.

If autism has been a blessing in my life, then shame has forever been my curse.

Now deep within me I can feel the fifteen-year-old boy, whose sadness was locked away in a mental institution for the most formative time of his life. I can feel his terror and extreme anxiety that was buried under an avalanche of powerful anti-psychotic medication.

At times I still wake in the early hours of the morning, my body dripping with sweat, my heart racing, terrified that I am back in that Victorian institution misdiagnosed and misunderstood. But now, thanks to my deeper understanding of myself, I revisit old wounds with gentleness and love. My diagnosis has given me permission to love myself.

Suffering cannot only break me down, it can also break me open, as long as I am willing and able to listen to those parts of myself that would have been previously unbearable to hear.

With the integrative process now well under way, all that had been resonating with me for so long is now resonating WITHIN me. There is no longer a split between different aspects of myself, all is breathing as one within me.

With such communion at depth I feel the enormity of my loss. The loss that is beyond words to express flows forth like an ocean of tears within me. At times I also feel anger and rage towards God. My anger tells me that I am real, that I am human and that my anguish can be held, affirmed and given a foothold, as the floodgates of grief so powerfully take me from meaninglessness to meaningfulness.

As Winnicott said – 'I am seen therefore I am.'

I hold no blame whatsoever towards my parents or sister for not recognising my autism, even though my father worked in the medical profession, as does my sister. Ignorance is easy for me to forgive, for the simple reason that I myself have remained so very ignorant of things of such fundamental importance throughout my life.

I would like to make it known that, although I have not held back in using strong terminology in conveying my childhood experiences, I have found it in myself to forgive my adoptive parents and also the doctor who sexually abused me, and I feel it of great importance to express what forgiveness means to me.

Forgiveness for me is not about forgetting, but about letting go of the hurt that previously held me hostage. Forgiveness and letting go of my pain go hand in hand. Feeling my feelings teaches me empathy for others. I was told once that forgiveness in Aramaic means to return to a natural state. I would like to be even more natural, for the forgiveness process never seems to end.

For me it is this emptying of and letting go of the pain which is the prerequisite to offering or expressing forgiveness to another. For me, to touch the essence of forgiveness I have to yield to a process of negation – that is, the grieving process. Right doing proceeds from right being, loving the enemy within (my shadow) in order to authentically offer real forgiveness. It seems to me that the abyss between good and evil is vast, but the bridge across it is only to be found within my own heart.

Today I give my time voluntarily, offering spiritual direction at the Spirituality Centre at Westminster Cathedral. Spiritual direction, or spiritual accompaniment as I prefer to call it, offers a space for people to observe inwardly all that is interfering with their true self, and in so doing one can be listened to at great depth. I would say that the process of receiving direction over the years, first from Patrick, and then in my own spiritual direction training, including my fortnightly sessions with my own director, have been instrumental in all that has led me to where I am now. And for that I am truly grateful.

In silence, and only in silence, am I able to move beyond my habitual reaction to a world that is naturally overwhelming for me, and thus break out of neurologically determined patterns that have woven their way into my very being. Consequently, the ministry of spiritual direction is a natural home for my gifts.

I also volunteer at the Catholic Worker community café in Hackney, East London, with my friends Father Martin, Zelda and Ciaron. In many ways the experience of being in the café is not too dissimilar to that of spiritual direction, in that the ethos of the worker is to create a space whereby the poor, marginalised, and vulnerable can be nourished and listened to. It is a place where people tell their stories and thus can be truly themselves. It is a great joy for me to be a part of this community, although it can also be a very overwhelming environment for me to be in too.

Therefore I have now arranged to use a quiet room within the crypt, but separate from the café, where I can offer spiritual direction, in keeping with the beautiful philosophy of Dorothy Day and the Catholic Worker movement.

Since my diagnosis with Asperger's syndrome, people who know me at the Catholic Worker are now able to understand why it was in the past I rarely attended meetings or participated fully in community activities. In a sense they are teaching me to teach people what my needs are. This is very new to me. This is very exciting.

I end with a quotation from one of Thomas Merton's literary essays. I feel it speaks to me of my deepest nature.

> *Alienation begins when culture divides me against myself, puts a mask on me, and gives me a role I may or may not want to play. Alienation is complete when I become completely identified with my mask, totally satisfied with my role, and convince myself that any other identity or role is inconceivable. The man who sweats under his mask, whose role makes him itch with discomfort, who hates the division in himself, is already beginning to be free. But God help him if all he wants is the mask the other man is wearing, just because the other one does not seem to be sweating or itching. Maybe he is no longer human enough to itch.*

Postscript

As I write the end to my story, I have just heard the news that a well-known and well-loved author of many books on autism, who herself had Asperger's syndrome, has committed suicide. She had spent much of her life struggling with ongoing bouts of depression. For many high-functioning autistics, depression and anxiety can seem almost inevitable consequences of attempting to live as full a life as possible.

It is a cruel fact that our intellectual and philosophical gifts can at times take us to a well we can never truly nor deeply drink from. When life itself becomes that well, depression is inevitable, and without understanding, compassion and gentleness towards ourselves, we can become deeply lost. Life can become unbearable and unendurable.

Having been in touch with others like myself who were diagnosed with Asperger's syndrome later in life, it is clear that it can be an overwhelming blow for many of us.

Our sense of self can be totally shattered, leaving us with a complex grieving process on top of an identity crisis, as a result of the dramatic end to our over-identification with our adaptive self. The need for specialists in this re-integration process is great indeed, and I hope that my book can play some part in illuminating the hearts and minds of professionals working in this area of autism in the future.

The well that sustains me in this life is Jesus. I knew that, throughout all my trials outlined in this story, I was not completely alone, that there was one who had been before me, enduring all that he did for my sake. Jesus' story and the Stations of the Cross offer me not only a way of understanding my suffering, but also a way of transcending it.

I feel deeply that healing starts for me when I am able to move from *my* pain to *the* pain, when I am able to realise that my own pain is a share in humanity's pain. For me, there is no better example of this than the Stations of the Cross.

As the pain of unknowing is transformed into the pain of knowing, I can see that although I am poor, and have little material security to offer myself or my son, I have the comfort of knowing that I have not let anxiety win. At times, my fortnightly visits to my son have been like a blind man walking into a field of battle, with nothing but the intense fire of love in my heart and my love of Jesus to see me through.

Understanding my wounds can only be healing, when that understanding is put at the service of the heart. 'Living my wounds through', as Henri Nouwen would say. This involves letting go of many questions such as, 'Why was I neglected as a child?' 'Why, seen in material terms, has my sister become a success in the world and I have become a failure?' There is no comfort to be found in such questions – they offer me a little distance from my pain, but will not help me in coming through the other side into the light of resurrection.

I feel deeply that the suffering of Jesus is the suffering of all humanity. As I have, said healing comes when I realise that my own particular pain is a share in humanity's pain. It is important for me to say this because I feel my pain takes me out of my isolation and links me to the world I always felt alienated from.

Could there be a greater joy than to feel this feeling of deep unity with humanity? Could it be that the shattering of the illusion that we are separate from each other can only come about through great love and great suffering? Perhaps many of us fear our spiritual and mystical nature, because we fear our shadow and the terrible tension in ourselves that goes with having to accept that the most despised and outcast in our midst reside in our own heart.

To wake to this reality is a wonderful thing indeed. To see myself and humanity as one whole unified body, and that those parts of the body that are weak and broken are to be respected, valued and treasured. To see difference in this way helps me to view my life no longer in terms of neglect or misfortune, or for that matter to measure my worth in terms of worldly success. What is of far greater importance for me are the questions, 'How much have I loved?' and 'How much have I forgiven?'

As a spiritual director and Alexander technique teacher, I feel I am now in a position of greater authenticity and depth to accompany others into the deserts of their hearts, whether in the context of autism or otherwise. My greatest hope is that I can be of service to others through the fruits of my suffering.

Contact details

Chris Goodchild
www.chrisgoodchild.com

London Catholic Worker
www.londoncatholicworker.org.uk

National Autistic Society Helpline 0845 070 4003
www.autism.org.uk

Missing Link Support Services
www.missinglinksupportservice.co.uk

London Autistic Rights Movement
larm2008@gmail.com

Aspie Village
www.aspievillage.org.uk

Wrong Planet
www.wrongplanet.net

Aspergers Parallel Planet
www.asplanet.info

www.donnawilliams.net

www.auties.org

www.selfinexile.com

www.meetup.com/sweetalk

About the Artist

Julie Lonneman

Cincinnati artist Julie Lonneman has employed her talents in service to the Church since 1978, first as an art director and graphic designer, and now as a freelance illustrator. Her work graces the covers of many books and newsletters, and regularly appears in magazines such as *America*, *Sojourners*, and *St. Anthony Messenger*. She is the author of *Clip Art for Sundays and Solemnities*, published in 2003 by Liturgy Training Publications of Chicago. Julie has recently completed an art library of over 250 images for Augsberg Fortress Press.

All but three of the illustrations in this book were taken from her two sets of pictures 'Women's way of the cross' and her 'Scriptual way of the cross'. To these she added two extra ones to illustrate the first and second falls. The cover picture and the picture for Station 15 is called "Journey".

She can be reached at jlonneman@cinci.rr.com